Illustrations by Charlotte Lance

by Caren Trafford

POWer OUR WORLD...

MEET THE RENEWABLES

MEET THE MOB

MUZBAR

Our intergalactic space detective
has accepted a new mission:
to switch on and come clean.
Are you ready to power up and
give carbon a break?

WASU

Sometimes a bit of a drip.
Mostly goes with the flow;
loves MAJOR HOLS.

*Many Amazing Journeys over Rivers,
Hills, Oceans, Lands and Seas.*

CORN-COB

Recently promoted to kernel in
the Renewable mob. Loves motor
engine sports.

POO-LOOTER

Overworked and in need of a long
holiday. This old fossil just can't
get away. Can you help?

HOT-STUFF

Energetic, can flare up easily.
Always at the centre of things.
Likes a good fry-up and
never leaves anything half-baked.

WUNG-WUNG

Creating power blows him away!
Breezes in, but never gets out of
breath.

HOT-ROCK

Hard-headed, enjoys caving but can
get heated under pressure. Delivers a
punch when steamed up.

CONTENTS   P

Energy—where does it
come from?
Power up the Sun
How much can you use?
Power plants
Facts on Coal, Oil, Gas
Electricity explained
Power-station workings
News on Fossil Fuels
Non-Renewable energy
Meet the Renewables
Renewables in History
Hydro Power
Marine Power
Bio-Energy
Geothermal
Wind
Solar
Disappearing Act
Pay to Take Away
People Power
Work Together

Published by Etram Pty Ltd
www.planetkids.biz

First published in Australia
2008
Copyright
Text © Caren Trafford 2008 &
Illustrations © ETRAM 2008
All rights reserved.
No part of this publication may be
reproduced, stored in a retrieval
system, or transmitted in any
form or by any means, electronic,
mechanical, photocopying,
recorded, or otherwise, without
the prior written permission of the
copyright owner.

National Library of Australia
Cataloguing-in-Publisher entry:
Trafford, Caren
POW! Meet the Renewables
ISBN 978-0-9581878-4-8

Illustrator: Charlotte Lance
Design: Bernadette Gethings
Printed in China through
Bookbuilders

ENERGY PACKS A POWERFUL PUNCH

Got a job or want stuff done?
Need a hand to push things along?
What can't be made? Won't go away?
Is invisible, but never out of sight?

The mightiest force you'll ever meet.
Full of get-up and go,
it's hard to beat. Always
ready: switched on or
standing by, it'll never
leave you high and dry.

Muzbar here… just
whizzed in to work
out what's a watt,
what's hot and
what's not. It's time
to shine the light on
ENERGY.

Where does it come
from? Mostly straight
from the Sun. Without
the Sun, there'd be no
heat, light or food. Nothing
would work, grow or even exist.

Feel energetic? Here's the chat.
Use it or move it… heat it or eat it…
Run, have fun… just bring it on…
Energy is Number One!

Every bright spark knows there's no stopping Energy:
it's always at work. Ever since it kick-started the
Universe - with a Big Bang!

Flick the Switch
40,000 times hotter than boiling water, dinner
would be cooked instantly if you lived on the Sun.

3

THE HEAT IS ON

Smack-bang in the middle of our Solar System the Sun has always been at the centre of attention. Planets, asteroids, meteoroids, comets and dust clouds all circle or *orbit* this huge ball of burning energy. From down here, the Sun might look like an old soccer ball, but it's full of gas and plasma. *Know anyone else like that?*

Prehistoric and ancient cultures worshipped the Sun as the *bringer of fire and light*. Today, we know it's the main source of energy for the Earth.

It's BIG - 100 times wider than this planet: you could fit one million Earths inside it!

It's DENSE - 99 times heavier that the rest of the solar system put together.

It's a STAR - emitting its own light and energy. Planets only reflect light and heat, so the Sun is the nearest star to planet Earth.

It's OLD - about 4.6 billion years old and still blazing bright.

It's HOT - but not the same temperature throughout. The outer layers are mega hot, but at the core, it's cooler. *You'd still need a hat and sun-block if you plan to visit.*

Some stars think everything revolves around them

Power Up
Almost 150 million kilometres away from Earth, the Sun's energy turns to heat when it hits things. That's why it's cooler in the shade.

What's it made of? Believe it or not, two of the lightest gases in the universe; hydrogen 70% and helium 28%. When hydrogen atoms collide together, they turn into helium, in an atomic reaction called *fusion*. These amazing cosmic collisions create huge explosions which generate the Sun's light, heat and energy.

The Earth is so small that only a tiny amount of the Sun's light hits the planet's surface but that contains enough energy to power the weather, climate and life.

The Sun is a middle-aged star, almost half-way through its life. It has enough hydrogen gas fuel to burn brightly for another five billion years. When that's all used up the Sun will start to burn up helium and expand, growing to about 100 times its current size: changing from a *yellow dwarf* into a *red giant*.

Once the helium runs out, the Sun will collapse into something quite small - a white dwarf.

How do you think the Sun likes its eggs? Boiled, poached, or sunny-side up?

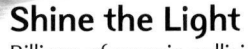

Shine the Light
Billions of cosmic collisions inside the Sun fuel its energy. In one second, the Sun produces more energy than the total ever used.

LAYERS OF SUNSHINE

The Sun has three visible layers.

The bright surface at the centre or core is the **photosphere.**

Surrounding the photosphere is the bright, red light of the **chromosphere**.

The **corona** is the outer layer appearing as a very thin, ghostly white halo. Reaching out 800,000 km, it's the hottest part of the Sun.

Sunspots are patches of disturbance on the Sun's surface, many times bigger than the Earth. Chinese astronomers noticed them about 2,800 years ago.

In 1612, **Galileo**, an Italian astronomer, used sunspots to prove the Sun rotates.

Sunspots create **solar flares** which heat to millions of degrees and release gigantic explosions. These send out x-rays and magnetic fields that hit the Earth as geomagnetic storms and solar winds, disrupting power-grids and radio transmissions and creating the **aurora borealis** – *the planet's greatest light-show.*

HOW MUCH CAN YOU USE?

The Sun's energy powers modern life along.

Imagine living without electricity or fuel. Your day would be very different - no hot food, cold drinks, computers, cars, cell-phones or CDs. Power is hugely popular and it's used up at a humungous rate.

In the last 200 years, more power has been used than in the previous 40,000 years.

*Feeling peckish,
want a bite?
When it's dark can you
turn on the light?
Late for school, do you need a ride?
It helps with Energy at your side.*

Guess where 80 percent of today's energy comes from? The answer's buried beneath your feet. Below the surface of the Earth lie vast supplies of trapped energy.

*How did it all get there?
It was created by the Sun,
millions of years ago.*

Don't you ever feel like getting unplugged?

As the world population increases, billions of tonnes of potential energy in the form of fossil fuels – *coal, oil and natural gas* – are mined, extracted and processed, to power homes, run industry, support communities and drive transport. Today, the flick of a switch will power up planet Earth, anytime day or night.

POWER PLANTS

Fossil fuels come from the plants and animals that lived hundreds of millions of years ago. Back then, warm algal-rich seas and swampy humid forests, sucked up the carbon-dioxide in the atmosphere and replaced it with oxygen.

As the huge trees, prehistoric plants, fish and insects died, they sank deep below layers of mud, rock, sand and water. Over millions of years, these buried plants and animals decomposed and turned into today's fossil fuels.

Coal, oil and gas are fossil fuels that come from the remains *or fossils* of prehistoric plants and animals. A little like a lucky dip, what they turned into depended on: who they were buried with, how long they were buried, how hot it got and the sort of pressure they were put under.

But whichever way they ended up, all of them were potential energy, waiting to be discovered.

MEET THE FOSSILS

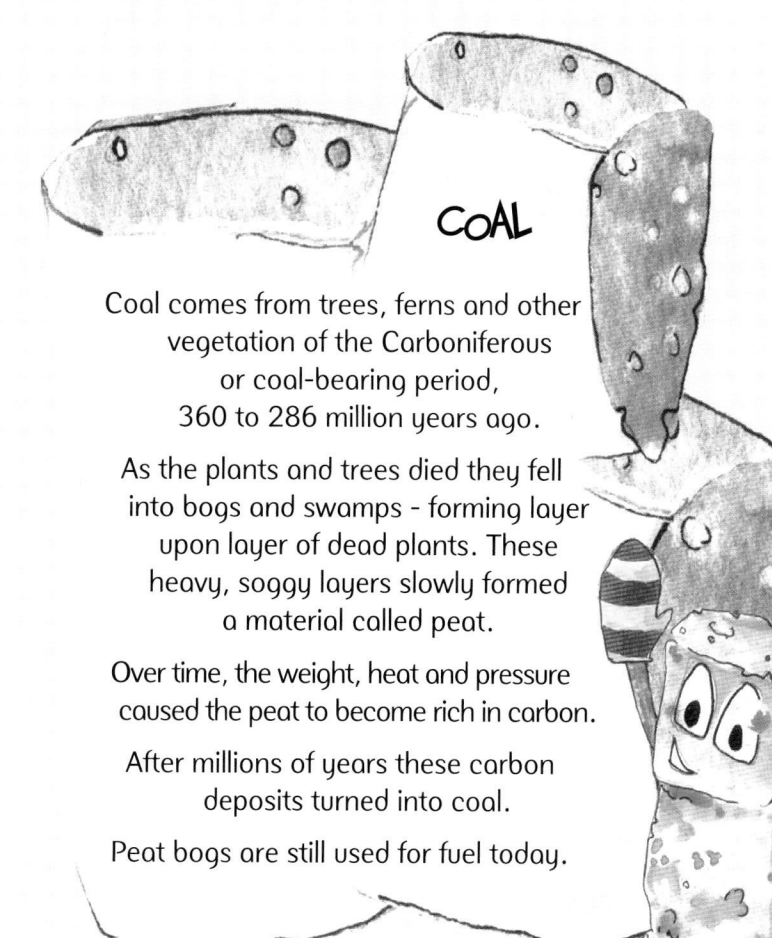

OIL
aka Petroleum

and Natural Gas come from protoplankton: minute, single-celled life-forms, found in the oceans.

When these tiny marine organisms died, they mixed with the mud and sand on the ocean floor.

Over millions of years, heat and pressure cooked this organic soup into a dark, waxy substance called kerogen.

This mixture eventually turned liquid or gassy – today's oil or natural gas.

Once covered by seas, today's Middle Eastern deserts produce 2/3rds of the world's oil.

COAL

Coal comes from trees, ferns and other vegetation of the Carboniferous or coal-bearing period, 360 to 286 million years ago.

As the plants and trees died they fell into bogs and swamps - forming layer upon layer of dead plants. These heavy, soggy layers slowly formed a material called peat.

Over time, the weight, heat and pressure caused the peat to become rich in carbon.

After millions of years these carbon deposits turned into coal.

Peat bogs are still used for fuel today.

ENERGY MATTERS

COAL

Coal is the world's most abundant and widely used fossil fuel. It's made from carbon, hydrogen, oxygen, nitrogen and sulphur.

The three main types of coal are anthracite, bituminous and lignite. *Anthracite* is the hardest - shiny black with high carbon content. It burns with the cleanest flame. *Lignite* - brown coal - is the softest and wettest: low in carbon but high in hydrogen and oxygen. *Bituminous* is in-between.

25% of world energy and 40% of world electricity is generated by coal.

70% of world steel production depends on coal. Coal use is expected to increase by 43% between 2000 and 2020. *International Energy Agency*

Burning coal produces about 9 billion tonnes of carbon dioxide each year, plus pollutants such as sulphur dioxide and nitrogen oxides.

Electricity produced from coal is only 35% efficient. The rest is lost as unused heat.

Relaxing can be more energetic than it looks

OIL

The oil used today was formed between 150-200 million years ago.

Crude oil is a smelly, yellow-to-black liquid, usually found in underground sandstone or limestone reservoirs. It may be as thin as petrol (gasoline) or as thick as tar.

Potential oil wells are found by examining rock samples. The 'oil window' is typically 4–6 km below ground.

The world's top five crude oil-producing countries are: Saudi Arabia, Russia, the USA, Iran and China.

In ancient times, oil seeping up through the ground was used to waterproof boats and baskets and for paints, lighting and medicine.

Oil powers transport and is also used in more than 3,000 other products, such as fertilisers, clothes, most plastics, ink, bubble gum, dishwashing liquid and tyres.

Burning oil produces nitrogen oxides, sulphur dioxide, carbon dioxide, methane and other pollutants.

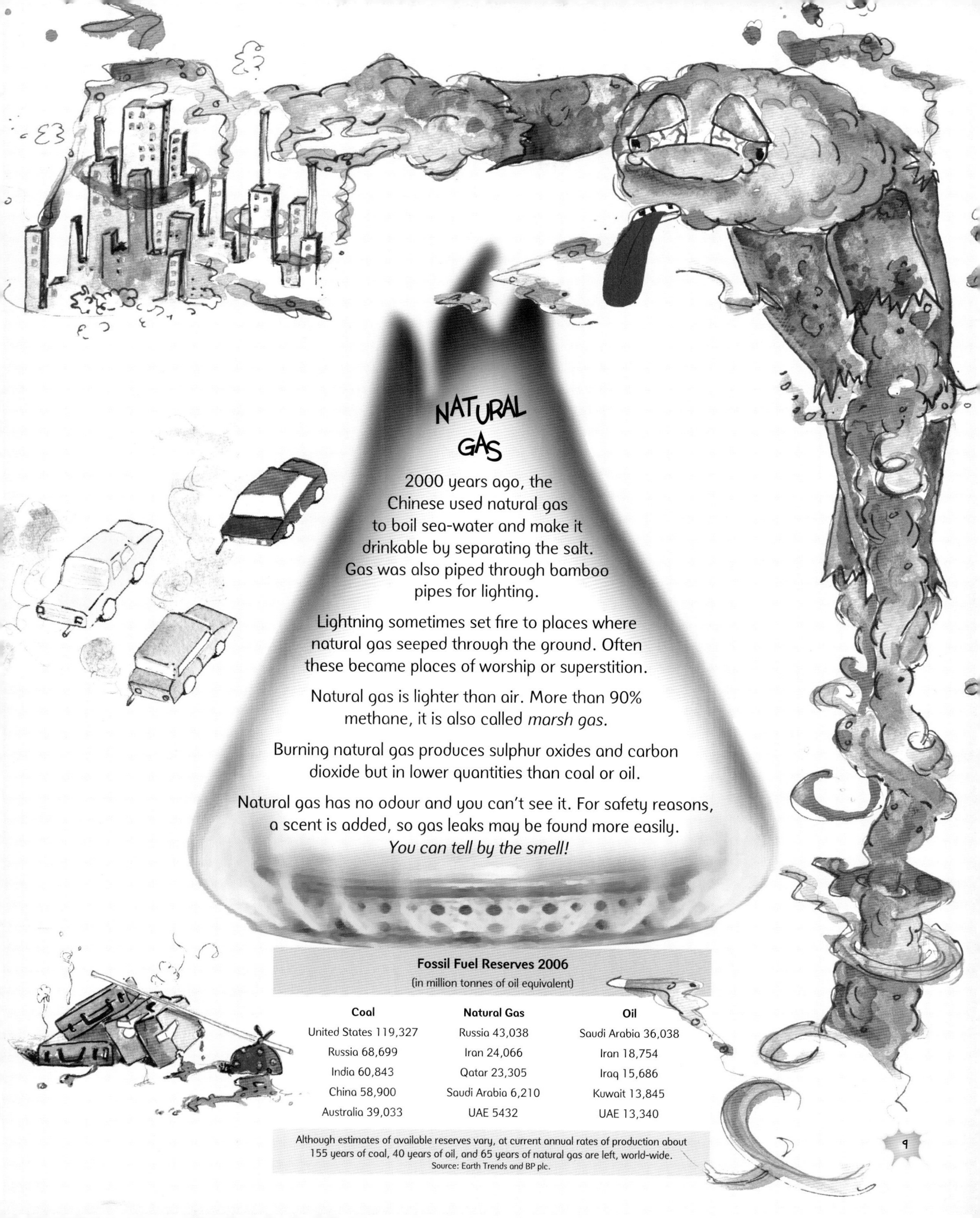

NATURAL GAS

2000 years ago, the Chinese used natural gas to boil sea-water and make it drinkable by separating the salt. Gas was also piped through bamboo pipes for lighting.

Lightning sometimes set fire to places where natural gas seeped through the ground. Often these became places of worship or superstition.

Natural gas is lighter than air. More than 90% methane, it is also called *marsh gas*.

Burning natural gas produces sulphur oxides and carbon dioxide but in lower quantities than coal or oil.

Natural gas has no odour and you can't see it. For safety reasons, a scent is added, so gas leaks may be found more easily. *You can tell by the smell!*

Fossil Fuel Reserves 2006
(in million tonnes of oil equivalent)

Coal	Natural Gas	Oil
United States 119,327	Russia 43,038	Saudi Arabia 36,038
Russia 68,699	Iran 24,066	Iran 18,754
India 60,843	Qatar 23,305	Iraq 15,686
China 58,900	Saudi Arabia 6,210	Kuwait 13,845
Australia 39,033	UAE 5432	UAE 13,340

Although estimates of available reserves vary, at current annual rates of production about 155 years of coal, 40 years of oil, and 65 years of natural gas are left, world-wide.
Source: Earth Trends and BP plc.

WHO'S A BRIGHT SPARK?

Electricity is the key to our modern world. Flick a switch, turn a key, push a plug or twist a dial and POW... ZAP... electricity. Electricity is made from tiny sub-atomic particles called electrons. You can't see them, but they zip around and light up your life. *Awesome...*

Furnace: Fuel, mostly coal, oil or gas, is burned in a giant furnace.

Boiler: Released heat boils water into steam.

Turbine: Steam under pressure turns a wheel called a turbine, *like a windmill*, made of tightly packed metal blades. The blades convert the steam's energy into moving or *kinetic* energy.

Generator: The turbine is linked to a generator. As the turbine spins, it turns the generator, transforming kinetic energy into electricity.

Cooling tower: Hot water from the turbine is cooled in giant towers and pumped back for re-use. 2/3rds of the heat produced in fossil fuel power-stations escapes in the cooling towers or is lost along the transmission lines.

Electric cables: Electricity travels from the generator along transmission lines or cables to a transformer.

Step-up transformer: Electricity loses energy as it travels: high-voltage electricity loses less energy than low-voltage so it's stepped-up to a very high voltage when leaving the power-station.

WHAT's a WATT?

Volts: measure electrical pressure. Voltage is the force that pushes electricity along.
Amps or Ampere: the unit of measurement for an electric current.
Joules: the energy needed to move an object. One **joule** is produced when one **amp** flows through one **volt**. **Joules** per second = **Watts**.
Watts: Electricity is measured in watts.

THERE'S POWER AT THE STATION

Lightning is natural electricity, released when electrical charges build up during thunderstorms. Clever humans have learnt how to make their own electricity. The electricity flowing into your home, school, TV, computer and toaster usually starts its life at a power-plant or power-station.

Pylons: Huge metal towers carry electricity at extremely high voltages along overhead cables, to where it's needed.

Step-down transformer: Once the electricity reaches its destination, another transformer converts it back to a lower voltage.

Homes: Electricity flows into homes through underground or overhead cables. Homes receive energy from coal-fired or renewable energy power-stations or a mixture of both.

A **meter-box** measures how much electricity is used. For safety, fuses or circuit breakers are built in, to cut the electricity supply if necessary.

Electricity flows around your home through wires attached to plugs on the wall.

Electricity cannot be stored - it must be used when it's generated. Different amounts are produced as seasons change and at different times of day.

80 percent of power - stations burn fossil fuel to create power.

WHAT's Hot and WHAT's Not?
Lightning can contain 30 million volts. It strikes the Earth about 8 million times a day.
Electric Eels generate 650 volts – *there's a big choice* – about 69 different species.

GOING UP IN SMOKE

Why have fossil fuels become so popular? Simple! You can dig or drill for them, store them easily and when you burn them they produce power, effortlessly.

The bad news is that burning fossil fuels sends billions of tonnes of extra Greenhouse Gas gang members into the atmosphere. These extra gases block the Sun's rays, stop heat from escaping and warm up the planet. *It's like adding blankets.*

The news gets worse. There is a 90 percent likelihood that the release of these extra GHGs causes longer droughts, more flooding-rains and severe heat-waves.

Have you ever heard a snoring sun-beam?

There's still more bad news. Polluting oxides are released when fossil fuels are burnt. These turn rain to acid, fill the air with smog, kill lakes and forests, and cause lung damage and breathing problems.

Burning fossil fuel creates air pollution that kills thousands of people each year. Often the air pollution manufactured in one country travels quite freely and affects environments vast distances away: nowhere is safe.

Would anyone like some planet with their main course?

Oh… one more thing.

Right now, the world economy is dependent on fossil fuels, so it might be a good time to mention:
fossil fuels are running out.

12

NON-RENEWABLE NUMBERS

The USA, China and the EU, consume more than 50% of all fossil fuel used each year.

In 2004, fossil fuel trade totalled US$715 billion world-wide.
World Bank, 2006.

Australia, China, Poland and South Africa, produce more than 75% of their electricity from coal-fired generators.

India relies on coal for 60% of its electric power. USA and Germany burn coal to supply more than half their electricity.

Nuclear energy provides 16% of the world's electricity. 80% of France's and 20% of the USA's electrical energy comes from nuclear power.

DO THE MATHS

Sunshine, water, minerals, air, plants, animals and soil are all natural resources. Some natural resources are renewable, meaning they can be replaced, but others are non-renewable and cannot be replaced as quickly as they are used.

Fossil fuels are non-renewable resources: they take millions of years to create and when they're used up, they'll be gone.

Nuclear energy is another non-renewable resource, used to create power. Ore called yellowcake is extracted from Uranium. *No... you can't eat it*. Atoms are split in a process called *fission*. Nuclear power-stations use the heat from fission to boil water into steam, to run generators and create electricity.

What about wood? Burning wood has been a source of energy since people first lived in caves. Unfortunately in many parts of the world, forests are disappearing more quickly than they can be replanted.

Some classes are more popular than others

ADD IT UP

Electricity demand is increasing and is likely to almost double from 2004 to 2030.
OECD 2006

By 2030, energy demand will have increased over 50% and CO_2 emissions by 52%, if policies remain unchanged.
World Energy Outlook 2005

Today, more than 80 percent of energy is created by fossil fuel and the other non-renewables.

Wouldn't it be great to find a way to produce power that didn't create *poo-lootion* or send extra members of the Greenhouse Gas gang into the atmosphere: a source of energy that would never run out?

Believe it or not, there's a source of energy just like that... *meet the Renewables*.

MEET THE RENEWABLES

Renewable or sustainable energy is all around you. Nature has been using *and renewing* energy for millions of years.

Renewable power sources come in many forms: water, sun, wind, hot rocks and organics are all part of the team. These power sources ran the energy show, until fossil fuels were discovered in large quantities during the 19th century.

What's so great about Renewable energy supplies?

They don't contribute to climate change or global warming,
>won't upset the weather,
>>won't run-out,
don't add pollutants like smog, acid rain or the GHG gang to the atmosphere and are always around, with a clean act, waiting to be switched on…

Renewables have been around since the planet was in nappies

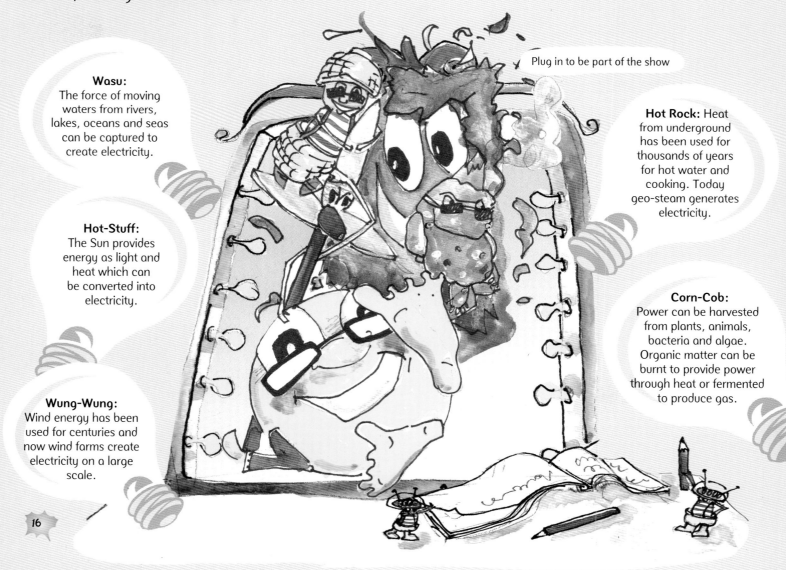

Plug in to be part of the show

Wasu:
The force of moving waters from rivers, lakes, oceans and seas can be captured to create electricity.

Hot-Stuff:
The Sun provides energy as light and heat which can be converted into electricity.

Wung-Wung:
Wind energy has been used for centuries and now wind farms create electricity on a large scale.

Hot Rock: Heat from underground has been used for thousands of years for hot water and cooking. Today geo-steam generates electricity.

Corn-Cob:
Power can be harvested from plants, animals, bacteria and algae. Organic matter can be burnt to provide power through heat or fermented to produce gas.

ENERGY-MAKING HISTORY

Renewable energy sources could supply enough energy for everyone but today they provide only seven percent of the world's power: the rest comes from fossil fuels and nuclear power. History shows it wasn't always this way:

SUN

· Ancient Greeks designed whole cities to catch the Sun's rays in winter - early solar heating.
· Romans used glass to trap the Sun's heat and grow exotic fruits and veggies.
· In ancient Persia, *Iran*, the Sun heated air in tall chimneys which brought up cool air from underground to 'air-condition' buildings.

WATER

· Ancient Egyptians planted and irrigated their crops according to tidal surges.
· Early civilisations in China and Egypt used large waterwheels to lift river-water, irrigate fields and supply the cities with drinking-water.
· More than 1,000 years ago, tide mills were used to mill grain on the Spanish, French and British coasts.

GEOTHERMAL

· Ancient Romans used hot springs for bathing and home heating.
· 10,000 years ago, North American Paleo-Indians used hot springs for cooking. Areas around the hot springs were neutral zones; weapons were not allowed so warriors could bathe together in peace!

WIND

· 5,000 years ago, the Egyptians sailed ships powered by the wind.
· Windmills have been used for centuries to grind grain and lift water.
· In Holland, windmills pumped water to stop flooding.
· *Windcatchers* in the Middle East, provided natural ventilation.

BIO-FUEL

· Wood is the oldest bio-fuel. It just took a while to 'invent' fire.
· In Persia, 700 years ago, bio-gas was captured from underground sewage systems for street lighting and to heat water.
· In the Middle Ages, dung cakes were sold for the same price as wood or charcoal.

POUR IN THE POWER

Water droplets are always on the move. MAJOR HOLS means water can travel all over the planet for FREE and thanks to gravity, every water droplet is bursting with liquid energy.

HYDRO POWER

Hydro-power is the world's largest renewable resource, producing about 20% of world electricity.

Hydro means water. Top hydro-energy producers: Norway 99%, Brazil 80%, New Zealand 70%, Canada 62% and Switzerland 57%. Hydro-electricity produces no direct Greenhouse gases, pollution or waste.

Dams store water, so energy is available year round. Once a dam is built and paid for, the energy is virtually free.

Hydro-electric power stations can produce power very quickly by using water stored above the power station.

High rainfall areas in steep mountains are perfect places to collect or harness the energy inside water. Treat them nicely and *POW...WOW...* water droplets will produce hydro-electric power.

Water droplets have been putting pressure on water-wheels, pushing them around for centuries.

Ever met a water droplet who didn't like to rain down on a parade?

Hydro-electric power is produced from the pressure of water droplets flowing downhill through huge pipes and pushing against enormous turbine blades, making them turn. The turbines connect to generators which spin and create electricity. *It's easy when you know how...*

A modern hydro-power station converts over 90 percent of water-energy into electricity: *you can even drink the water afterwards!*

Smaller or mini hydro power-stations catch the natural flow of the river to make power. These are ideal for people living in isolated areas; they can use water-power, instead of running petrol or diesel generators.

The hydro-flow is a great ride but some water-droplets prefer to walk

ENERGY TO SHORE - COME IN PLEASE

Oceans cover 70 percent of the Earth's surface and are also full of energy on the move! The moon and wind whip up waves whilst the Sun heats the water, creating currents that move water around the planet.

Waves travel vast distances without getting tired so they are extremely effective energy-movers. When wave energy is caught, it can be converted into electricity.

How much coast-line is there? If only a tiny 0.2 percent of wave energy was captured, it could provide enough electricity for everyone: it's clean, mean and *sometimes makes you green*.

Avoid the traffic: go to work on the surf

POWER FROM THE DEEP

Energy harvested from the oceans could equal twice the amount of electricity currently produced.
World Energy Council

Wave energy has the potential to provide 10% of global electricity.

GO WITH THE FLOW

Tides are also full of energy. Moon-powered tides flow in and out twice a day, every day. That means billions of litres of moving water are ready to go with the flow. The motion of the ocean can carve continents, sink ships or cover islands and the motion of tides can be used to create electricity.

Tidal turbines are built along the same lines as wind turbines, but instead of wind, it's water that pushes and turns large turbine blades to generate power.

Bobbing buoys, nodding ducks, water columns and *giant sea-snakes* are a few great ways that water power-collectors turn waves, into watts.

Next time you visit the ocean, remember... waves love the surf and soon their clean, renewable energy might light your way home.

FLUSHED WITH SUCCESS

Nature has a green thumb - it loves growing things. Plants absorb energy from the Sun, through a process called *photosynthesis*. Bio-mass is organic material grown by Nature and it contains a vast amount of energy. Wood, dried animal do-do, fats and vegetable oils have been burnt for heat, light and hot water for many thousands of years.

Even Nature sometimes needs a hair-cut

GROW YOUR OWN

Biomass gas from sewage has been used for centuries for lighting and heating.

Since the 1940s, in India, over a million homes have cooked with gas from biomass.

Before World War II, the UK and Germany sold bio-fuels mixed with petrol.

Sugar-cane waste, *aka bagasse*, can be converted into electricity to run sugar mills.

New Zealand is selling bio-fuel created from dairy industry waste.

India has the world's largest cattle population, some 262 million: *that's a lot of gas!*

ENERGETIC WASTE

The *muck you chuck* and the *waste you create* can be turned into energy. Waste that is burnt provides heat and when fermented, it creates a gas that can power cookers, ovens, furnaces or generators. The woodchip, sugar-cane and dairy industries ferment much of their waste into fuel.

Energy comes from many sources - some more unusual than others

With biomass, it's easy to balance the books. Plants absorb the same amount of carbon from the soil and atmosphere as they release when used as a fuel.

Because biomass regrows when harvested, it's part of the Renewable energy mob. *You can grow it, mow it, sow it or hoe it. Power from sewage, waste, poo or animal do-do – it's up to you!*

POWER TO THE BURPS
Many animals, humans included, produce bottom burps or biogas when they digest food. Cows burp methane but tiny termites contribute more methane gas to the atmosphere than any other creature.

RUN YOUR CAR ON PEANUTS

Power your car, truck, scooter or boat with vegetable oils! All sorts of them!

Mr Diesel designed the original diesel engine in the late 1800s to run on peanut oil not fossil fuel.

Palm oil and soy bean oil are the most widely-used vegetable fuel oils but you could also use canola, sunflower and flax oil.

On your salad or in the car… that is the question.

You'll never run out of dressing when you take biogas on a picnic

FILLING THE TANK

Brazil, the USA, China and India are the largest ethanol producers.

The EU has agreed to replace 10% of its transport fuel with biofuels, including palm oil, by 2020.

From 2007, all diesel sold in Malaysia must contain 5% palm oil.

The USA has set a goal of replacing 30% of petrol *(gasoline)* with biofuels by 2030.

Renault, Saab, Toyota and Ford are designing vehicles to run on 100% ethanol.

GIVE YOUR CAR A DRINK

When Mr Ford designed the first Ford car, he thought it would be powered by ethanol. *Where does ethanol come from?* Plants! It's an alcohol made from corn, sugar-beet or sugar-cane and most cars happily run on it when it's mixed with traditional fuel.

Other biomass sources can also provide power. Algae from sewage and other wastes are being tested for oil.

Scientists are developing a new bio-fuel created from munching microbes which could one day power cars, trains and even planes.

Do you think munching microbes pay to ride in the fuel tank?

FULL STEAM AHEAD

The centre of the Earth is hot and the deeper you go, the hotter it gets. Geothermal energy rises more than 6,000 kilometres from the centre, or core, of the Earth. *There's heat beneath your feet.*

Most geothermal energy is located in an area called the *Ring of Fire*. Under the sea, circling the Pacific Ocean Basin and on the edge of one of the main **tectonic plates**, are a series of volcanoes and ocean trenches. This is ground-breaking territory where 90 percent of the world's earthquakes occur.

How do you capture energy from a volcano? Deep down underground, the rocks absorb heat from extremely hot, volcanic molten **magma** as it rises up from the Earth's core. Water seeping down from the surface sizzles as it's super-heated by hot rocks. If heated water gets trapped between rock layers, it can form a giant steamy geothermal reservoir that's sometimes three times hotter than boiling water. *What a great source of energy!*

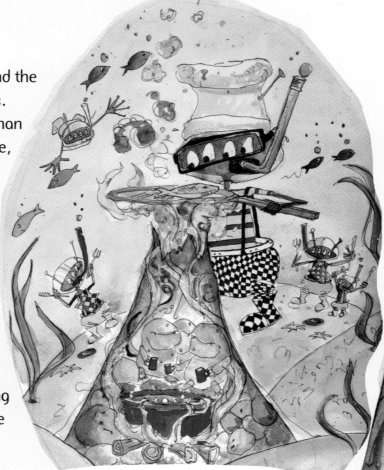

Under-water volcanoes save a lot of cooking time

Sizzling rocks are popular for steaming and cleaning

JOURNEY TO THE CENTRE OF THE EARTH

The Earth is made up of different layers:

At the centre is the **inner core**. It's a third of the size of the Moon and almost as hot as the Sun. It remains solid because of the enormous weight of the Earth around it.

The **outer core** is the next layer – made from molten iron, nickel and super hot melted rock called **magma.**

As the Earth rotates, the outer core spins around the inner core creating a **magnetic field**.

The **mantle** comes next. It's semi-molten and made from **magma** and rock.

The **crust** is the thin outer layer protecting everyone from the heat at the centre of the Earth.

The Earth's crust is broken into pieces called **tectonic plates** which can move and shift causing earthquakes and tsunamis.

Magma comes up close to the Earth's surface near the edges of these plates.

GETTING INTO HOT WATER

If no hot water is trapped in the reservoirs, extra holes are drilled and water from the surface is sent down to be heated by the hot rocks. It is then pumped back up to the surface as steam which powers turbines, heats homes or *you could fry your eggs in it*. This hot water can be recycled back down into the underground reservoirs and reused.

Geothermal power stations have been built all over the world: in deserts, tropical forests, woodlands or in the middle of farmland. They do not burn fuel or produce smoke.

If the geothermal water is not hot enough to produce electricity, it can still be used as a heat source. In Iceland and France, geothermal heat warms many public buildings, schools and homes.

In Iceland, geothermal energy heats pavements and roads to stop them from freezing in the winter.

95% of the buildings in Reykjavik, Iceland, are heated with geothermal water.

In New Mexico, rows of pipes carry geothermal water under the soil to help grow flowers or vegetables.

The agricultural industry uses geothermal energy to heat greenhouses, grow mushrooms and to wash and dry wool.

DIG DEEP, USE THE HEAT

From the Greek words, *geo* 'earth' and *therme* 'heat', geothermal electricity was first produced in Italy, in 1904.

Geothermal energy has great potential but produced only 0.5% of the world's electricity in 2005.

In South Australia, nearly 4 kms underground lies the hottest near-surface, non-volcanic rock ever discovered. It's potentially the largest geothermal resource in the world and contains enough heat to supply all of Australia's power for 75 years.

Iceland's government has proposed to drill almost 5 kms (3 miles) down into hot basalt and tap into temperatures of up to 600C. The intense heat could generate enough energy to power 1.5 million homes.

Feeling hot? There are many ways to chill out

WHO ARE YOU CALLING A WIND-BAG?

Wind never runs out of puff. Because the Sun heats the Earth's surface unevenly, warm air rises faster in some places than in others. Air can't stay still so cooler air rushes into the gaps, causing winds to blow.

As a power source, the winds have been used for many centuries. Sailors, explorers, farmers, millers, kite-flyers *and anyone who has ever hung the washing out to dry…* have all taken advantage of the power of the wind.

WINDS OF CHANGE

At the end of 2006, wind-power produced just over 1% of world-wide electricity. By 2010, this is set to increase to 2%.

Globally, wind-power generation more than quadrupled from 2000 to 2006.

China will be the biggest wind-power market within the next 5-8 years.

Less than 1% of land on a wind farm is taken up by wind turbines; the rest of the land could be used for other profitable purposes like farming.

Wind and water love working together. Tasmania, Australia, produces 95% of its electricity from these combined energy sources.

Many people living in the more remote regions of the world use wind-powered pumps to provide water and electricity. In Australia, in the 1930s and 1940s, isolated farms generated their own electricity from converted aeroplane propellers!

Some old props make more wind than others

Windmills have existed for thousands of years but wind farms are a more recent invention. Wind farms are built not to grow crops or run cattle, but to capture the wind's energy and convert it to electricity.

A modern wind farm is a series of tall towers that hold turbines high up in the air, allowing the wind to turn giant blades.

24 A wind turbine works the opposite way to a fan. Instead of using electricity to make wind, a turbine uses the wind to make electricity.

HOW BIG IS BIG ENOUGH?

When it comes to size, BIG is better. *Why?* The bigger the wind turbine, the more wind it can reach and therefore, the more electricity it will produce. Towers of steel, blades of fibre, magnets and copper wire: that's all it takes to turn wind into electricity. A typical turbine tower has three huge blades which rotate in the breeze. If there is too much wind, the rotor-blades switch off. One modern turbine can generate enough electricity for about 850 homes.

The biggest size wins the prize!

SHALL WE DANCE?

Wind farms don't have to be built on land. Denmark, has many offshore wind farms.

Wind-power is being blown ahead in leaps and bounds! It has the potential to be the leading renewable energy within the next ten to fifteen years, thanks to taller, quieter and more efficient wind turbines.

Next time you see a turbine turning with the wind, perhaps you'll also hear Nature playing their favourite tune?

The local dance is a great place to meet new friends

SUNNY-SIDE UP

The Sun's sizzling energy has been pouring down for millions of years but just over 50 years ago scientists discovered a way to create electricity from it. They invented photovoltaic cells using chemical elements like silicon which convert or transform the Sun's light energy into electrical energy. Today these cells power satellites, the international space station and much more.

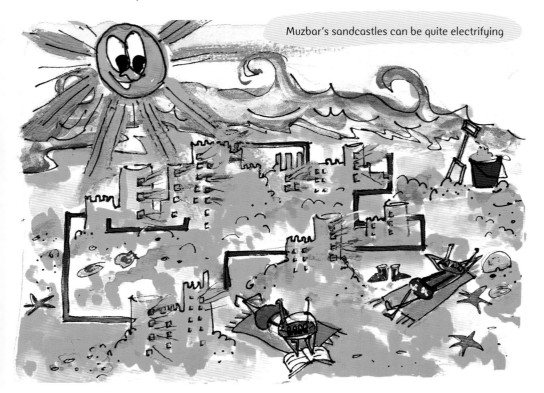

Muzbar's sandcastles can be quite electrifying

SUNNY TECHNOLOGY

In Greek, 'phos' means *light*, and 'voltaic', means *electrical*, from the name of the Italian physicist Volta. *Volts* are named after him.

Israel, China and India, are developing photovoltaic power stations to provide affordable energy for rural communities.

Germany, *where it rains a lot*, leads the world in the global solar industry.

Power Glass, is a new material based on photovoltaic panels that allows transparent glass windows to produce electricity from the Sun's energy.

Solar Clothes. In Japan a solar jacket has been developed that can power a mobile phone. Solar caps with an in-built fan will keep you cool.

World Solar Challenge is a solar-powered car race through Australia, designed to promote research on solar cars.

Photovoltaic cells are two layers of silicon wafers, sandwiched together. *You'll find silicon all over the Universe: it's in the stars, opals, your hair (even if it's curly) and your nails.* How do solar cells work? Sunlight charges the electrons in the silicon layers which push through wires and create electric currents.

Photovoltaic cells power plenty of products: watches, calculators, road-signs, parking-metres and *believe it or not,* clothes! New technology has found ways to create paper-thin photovoltaic cells, so they can be used on even more surfaces, like walls, tents, windows and parachutes.

Solar cells are especially useful in remote regions, where you can't connect to the electricity grid. Solar radios, telephones, lamps and ovens reduce the need for firewood and fossil fuel. If you have a roof, put a solar panel on it: you'll have heat, light and POWER - *just like magic!*

On some camping trips it's easy to phone home

WHAT A BRIGHT IDEA

The Sun's light is only one source of power; the Sun's heat is another. Solar thermal collectors can gather heat energy from the Sun to boil water or drive steam turbines and generate electricity.

Thermal solar power stations come in different shapes and sizes but they can all turn the Sun's heat into power.

The Tower: flat, moving mirrors track the Sun through the day. The heat is then focussed on the tower which houses tubes containing a liquid, *usually sodium*. This heats up enough to turn water into steam and power turbines.

Fancy a *Dish*? Large dish-shaped solar collectors are popular in small communities.

Sunlight can also be collected and mirrored with a *Parabolic Trough:* a long mirror, with a tube of oil running down the middle. A trough can focus the Sun at 30 to 100 times its normal intensity, heating the oil which powers a steam turbine.

Ever tried playing hide and seek with the Sun?

WHO'S FULL OF HOT AIR?

Air heated by the Sun can also generate electricity. A solar chimney works by sucking hot air upwards. The movement of the hot air spins turbines and creates electricity. This idea is based on the original ancient air-conditioners in super-hot desert countries: *always a cool idea.*

CHEAP – BUT WHAT'S THE COST?

Energy is the key to the developed world. Everything that's manufactured, transported, engineered, built, thrown out or recycled, relies on energy. 80 percent of world energy is still generated by fossil fuels.

When fossil fuels were discovered in large quantities, no-one realised how dirty they are to use and how much *poo-lootion* they release. By ignoring the cost of pollution, fossil fuel energy remained cheap.

How does food get to your table?
How are your clothes and shoes made?
Where do your books come from?

All this and much more is made possible thanks to dirty fossil fuel energy.

Does Poo-looter have our planet in the bag?

WHO'S GOT WATTS?

Two billion people, *almost one in three*, still have no electricity. Many of these people live in Africa, India and China, where large amounts of cheap fossil fuel energy; coal, oil and gas, are buried. If these nations want to improve their standard of living, they'll need to use energy – lots of it.

Renewable energy would be very happy to mop up

Remote, small villages could create electricity from renewable energy sources. Unfortunately, for most of these communities, this technology is too expensive. Until renewable energy technology becomes cheaper, developing countries will continue burning fossil fuel to generate energy.

China wants to produce 16 percent of its energy from renewable sources by 2020, but for now, a new coal power-station opens there, every ten days.

DON'T BE A FOSSIL

There's only ONE Earth. Unless you are an astronaut you can't move to another planet when this one fills up with waste and pollution from burning dirty fossils.

The *Intergovernmental Panel for Climate Change* reports that Greenhouse gas emissions are the probable cause for extreme changes in the weather. Droughts, intense storms, heatwaves, floods, global-warming; is the weather trying to tell you something?

It's time to clean up and reduce fossil fuel use. Here's how:

Scrubbing coal is one way to clean up

Price it right. Europe and Asia trade carbon and other GHG gang members. Companies sell or buy carbon debits and credits. Each carbon credit represents the removal of one tonne of CO_2 from the atmosphere.

Clean up Coal. It's the dirtiest fossil fuel. Wash or 'wet scrub' it to remove SOx or create an electric field to catch the polluting particles.

Cleaner Cars. Car numbers will double over the next 20 years. Hydrogen and hybrid cars reduce fossil fuel use.

Cut Energy use. Industry and business can be more energy-efficient just by turning out the lights when they go home at night! *Tell them!*

BE ENERGY SAVVY

People Power. Scientists say that energy from people walking can be turned into electricity. People power could light cities and drive electric trains. 84,162,203 footsteps could launch a space shuttle. *Start walking…*

Use the 'Rs'. Recycle, re-use, recover and rethink your waste to save energy.

Hydrogen is the most common element in the Universe. It can fuel your car and all your car produces is water.

Bio-batteries. A battery that uses sugar-water to produce power is being tested for the market. *How sweet is that?*

Where's the Money? World-wide more than $100 billion was invested in renewable energy in 2006, up from $80 billion in 2005. UN Report

…but there's still a long way to go…

CHANGING COURSE

How can you reduce global *poo-lootion?* Clean and green up and make way for efficient energy, at true planet prices. Simple actions make a difference.

DON'T WASTE ENERGY

Lighten Up. Use energy efficient light globes - they last longer and use much less energy.

Take a Hike. Walk, bike, use public transport, or car pool when possible. Form a walking bus. *You'd always have a seat by the window.*

Turn the dial. Moderate heating and cooling. Just a couple of degrees can make a big difference.

Use Nature. Dry your clothes with solar power. Open the window if you feel hot or close the doors to keep in the warmth.

Turn it off. If you're not using a light, the computer or the TV, turn them off! 'Standby' still consumes energy.

Think outside the square. Some companies now manufacture TVs and computers to automatically switch off when not in use. *What other inventions can you think of to save energy?*

How much do you need? Reusing and recycling saves energy, but you'll save even more if you don't use so much in the first place!

Get naked, buy local. Products without packaging and those grown or produced locally, have had far less energy spent to get them to your door than those shipped around the world.

MAKE THE SWITCH

KidzPower. Be a Nag. Tell your family and friends how to save energy. **Switch suppliers.** Buy your energy from renewable power sources. If enough people use clean energy, prices will drop. *Clean is green and fossils are mean.*

Get into hot water. Save money on heating and put a solar water heater or a solar panel on your roof.

WORK TOGETHER - POWER UP FOREVER

Your planet can offer you squeaky clean energy – it's up to you to take it and give Renewables a helping hand.

Are you energy savvy? Forget and forgive fossils and let poor *poo-looter* have the holiday he deserves.

The Renewable mob is standing by with all the clean energy you could ever need.

> *Fossil fuels have had their day...*
> *Renewables can point the way.*

For now, renewable energies will play their part alongside fossil fuels: two very different kinds of energy can work together, producing power, until YOU get smart and place the Renewables in the leading role.

They won't let you down - they've been creating energy for millions of years. Switch on your power:

*Don't just stand there, let's get to it, **P**ower* **O**ur **W**orld – *there's nothing to it.*